7

THE ORCHARD BOOK OF
VIKING STORIES

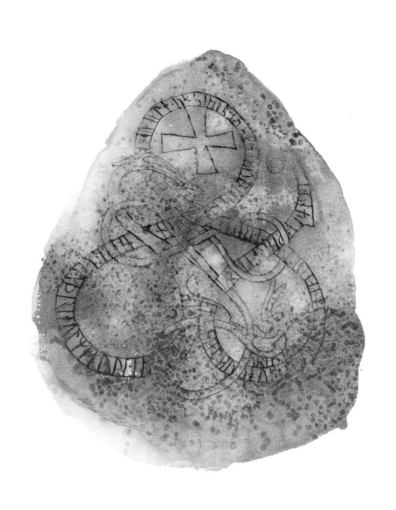

For Martin and Sinead
R S

To Jill Lambert, with love
S L

In the same series

THE ORCHARD BOOK OF GREEK MYTHS
Retold by Geraldine McCaughrean
Illustrated by Emma Chichester Clark

THE ORCHARD BOOK OF GREEK GODS AND GODDESSES
Retold by Geraldine McCaughrean
Illustrated by Emma Chichester Clark

THE ORCHARD BOOK OF ROMAN MYTHS
Retold by Geraldine McCaughrean
Illustrated by Emma Chichester Clark

THE ORCHARD BOOK OF STORIES FROM ANCIENT EGYPT
Retold by Robert Swindells
Illustrated by Stephen Lambert

THE ORCHARD BOOK OF LEGENDS OF KING ARTHUR
Retold by Andrew Matthews
Illustrated by Peter Utton

ORCHARD BOOKS
338 Euston Road, London NW1 3BH
Orchard Books Australia
Hachette Children's Books
Level 17/207 Kent Street, Sydney, NSW 2000
ISBN 1 84362 435 4
First published in Great Britain in 1999
This edition published in 2004
Text © Robert Swindells 1999
Illustrations © Peter Utton 1999
The rights of Robert Swindells to be identified as the author
and of Peter Utton to be identified as the illustrator
of this work has been asserted by them in accordance
with the Copyright, Designs and Patents Act 1988.
A CIP catalogue record for this book is available from the British Library.
3 5 7 9 10 8 6 4 2
Printed in Singapore

THE ORCHARD BOOK OF
VIKING STORIES

ROBERT SWINDELLS
ILLUSTRATED BY PETER UTTON

ORCHARD BOOKS

CONTENTS

CONTENTS

INTRODUCTION

THE VIKINGS or Northmen have always had a bad reputation in Britain. We tend to picture them as wild, ferocious raiders who came swarming out of their longships to slaughter, rape and burn: carrying off whatever took their fancy and leaving a trail of destruction in their wake. This is because our coastal settlements were sometimes subject to piratical assaults of this kind, but there was more to the Vikings than this. Far more.

The Northmen were farmers, explorers, craftsmen and storytellers, as well as conquerors. They settled in England, Scotland and Ireland, cultivating the soil and raising cattle, pigs and sheep. They made prodigious journeys of exploration by sea and over land, reaching the Black Sea to the east and the coast of what is now the USA to the west. As craftsmen they created beautiful zoomorphic designs which they carved in wood and stone. Their smiths produced similar designs in precious metals to make the most exquisite jewellery, and the ships and boats the Vikings built were the finest in the world.

The curiosity which drove the Northmen to go exploring also led them to wonder how the world was made and by whom.

Why do the sun and moon cross the sky, and what stops the sky from falling? What causes the wind to blow, why are there summers and winters, and where do we go when we die? There were very few scientists a thousand years ago to supply the true answers, so the Vikings made up stories to explain these wonders. They were stories of gods and goddesses, dwarfs and giants, dragons and serpents and wolves and wise old women.

These tales weren't written down, they were passed on through generations of storytellers and they were so ancient, even a thousand years ago, that nobody knew they were made up. Everybody believed them. Even when early Christian missionaries came with a different set of stories from the East, people clung to their beliefs and kept the old familiar stories alive in many languages till the age of the printed word, when they were written down at last. By then few still believed, but they were good stories and so they survived.

The Vikings are gone, but when we read these tales we sometimes catch a glimpse of them, just a glimpse, and for a moment perhaps we see the world through their eyes – its beauty and its wonder, which our scientific age has all but worn away.

HOW THE WORLD BEGAN

VIKINGS! Here is how the world began. Ice and fire. Ice was in Niflheim, far to the north. Ice and wind and endless snow. No creature lived in Niflheim. No creature could.

Fire was in Muspell, far to the south. Fire and smoke and lava streams, hotter than the sun. Nothing walked the searing plain of Muspell. Nothing grew.

Between Muspell and Niflheim yawned the bottomless void, Ginnungagap. The north part of Ginnungagap was fog and sleet and rotten ice, cracking and roiling and wuthering in perpetual agitation. The south part was a seething cauldron of thunder and boiling mud. And in Ginnungagap's middle, where cold and heat mingled, lay a region of steam and sodden air.

Muspell. Niflheim. Ginnungagap. Nothing else existed.

Then, somewhere in the steamy sodden heart of Ginnungagap, something began to grow. Something huge. It was made of ice and fire, fog and mud and brine, and gases that glowed and crackled, and it was *alive*. It stirred. Stirred and stretched with a sound like thunder, and hauled itself erect in the midst of the void. It was a giant – the first living thing – and its name was Ymir.

It was hot and sticky in that middle part of Ginnungagap. The giant sweated, and out of his sweat grew two more giants, a woman and a man. And one of Ymir's legs mated with the other and produced a son, and these three were the first Frost Giants.

Then, out of the same seething soup which had produced Ymir came the great cow Audumla. From her teats flowed four rivers of milk, and the frost giants fed from these while Audumla herself licked at the ice. As she licked and licked, the ice took on a manlike shape which breathed and moved and stood, and this was Buri, the first god. Ages rolled by while all of these events were taking place. Buri's son, Bor, married the daughter of a frost giant. Her name was Bestla. In due time Bestla bore three mighty sons: Odin, Vili and Ve. Now these three grew to hate the frost giants, and one day they waylaid Ymir in the fog and killed him.

It was a terrible slaying. So much blood spurted from the giant's wounds that the frost giants drowned in it, except Bergelmir and his wife, who rode the crimson sea in a tree-trunk boat.

When Ymir was dead, Odin, Vili and Ve hoisted his body on their shoulders and carried it to the middle of Ginnungagap. There they used its parts to create the world. His flesh became the earth and from his bones they made the mountains. His jaws and teeth were crags and boulders. The blood formed lakes and seas and the mighty oceans which surrounded all the land. And when all of this was done, the three mighty brothers lifted the dome of Ymir's skull so that it arched over all of the earth, and this became the sky. To fix it in position, the brothers placed a dwarf where each of its four corners touched the ground. These dwarfs support the sky, and their names are North, South, East and West. Then the brothers seized Ymir's brains and flung them into the sky they had made, where they became clouds.

In Muspell was fire. The mighty trio scooped up sparks and embers of this fire and flung them at the sky for sun, moon and stars, to shed light on the round earth and the ocean which surrounded it.

Next, the three brothers marked out a great stretch of land near the ocean as a home for the frost giants and the rock giants, and its name was Jotunheim. Here the descendants of Bergelmir settled, but they were so fierce and warlike that Odin, Vili and Ve didn't trust them, so they took Ymir's eyebrows and used them to enclose a great tract of land far away from Jotunheim, and this they called Midgard. And the rain fell gently on the soil of Midgard, and the sun warmed it, and a thousand thousand green things grew, so that Midgard became like a vast and beautiful garden.

One day, strolling on the seashore, the three brothers found two trees that had been torn up by their roots. One was an elm, the other an ash, and out of them the brothers fashioned the first woman and the first man, breathing life into them and giving them thoughts and feelings as well as sight and hearing. The woman's name was Embla and the man was called Ask, and the brothers took them to beautiful Midgard, where they settled. And all humans of every race are descended from Ask and Embla.

Meanwhile in Jotunheim a daughter was born to one of the giants. She had dark eyes, raven hair and a swarthy complexion, and her parents named her Night. Night grew up and married and in due course gave birth to a son. This child took after his father, being fair and golden-haired, and his mother called him Day. Now when Odin heard about Night and Day he mounted his horse, rode to Jotunheim and carried mother and son away. He put them into horse-drawn chariots and set them to gallop for ever across the sky. Night's horse is pale, with icy breath and a sparkling, frosty mane. Day's horse is bright like fire and lights up all the sky.

In Midgard lived a man whose name was Mundilfari. His wife bore him two children who were so beautiful that he called them Sun and Moon. Now when the offspring of Odin, Vili and

Ve, who are known as the Aesir, heard about this, they were angry. "What a *conceited* man this Mundilfari must be!" they growled. To punish him, they kidnapped Sun and Moon and placed them in the sky to guide the two chariots. Sun guides Day's chariot while Moon guides Night's. Both guides are grimly pursued by wolves. Sun's wolf is called Skoll, and he snaps and snarls so close that Sun seems always to hurry. Moon is hunted by Hati. In the end *both* wolves will catch their prey.

Presently, Odin, Vili and Ve recalled the vile maggots that had infested Ymir's flesh after his death. They found these maggots, gave them the wits and shapes of men, and made them live in caves and grottoes under the earth and inside hollow hills, and these are known as dwarfs.

The brothers' final task was to build a realm for themselves and the Aesir; a mighty citadel fit for gods to dwell in. They set this citadel high above Midgard and named it Asgard. Asgard was linked to Midgard by a flaming rainbow bridge called Bifrost, so that the Aesir can cross the bridge and visit Midgard or Jotunheim whenever they want to.

And there they live: twelve divine gods, twelve divine goddesses and all of the Aesir. This was the beginning of all that has happened and will happen, throughout the world.

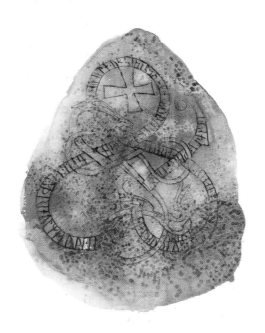

SHAPE-CHANGER
Loki and the walls of Asgard

A QUARREL broke out among the gods in Asgard. Nobody would back down, so the quarrel became a row and the row led to war. War between gods is a fearsome thing, the cause of unimaginable destruction. In this war the mighty wall which surrounded Asgard was utterly destroyed. And when, after a long time, the gods grew sick of fighting and decided to live in peace with one another, they wanted the wall rebuilt. Trouble was, none of the war-weary gods fancied tackling such an enormous job. Time passed. The wall stayed a ruin. The wind blew seeds into its cracks, so that plants sprouted among the rubble. Birds nested between the smashed boulders. Asgard lay unfortified.

One day, a man on horseback came cantering over the rainbow bridge. Heimdall the watchman stopped him. "What's your business in Asgard?" he demanded.

"I've come to talk to the gods," the horseman replied. "I have a plan to put to them." Heimdall allowed him to pass, and he rode on till he came to a great hall called Gladsheim, where the gods and goddesses were assembled. He dismounted and strode into the hall.

Odin glared at him. "Heimdall told us to expect you," he rumbled. "What d'you want?"

"I can rebuild the wall round Asgard," the man replied. "I can make it even better than it was before. It will be so strong, Asgard will be safe from rock giants and frost giants for ever."

"Hmmm!" growled Odin. "And what's the catch?" He knew the builder would want something special by way of payment.

"No catch," said the man. "The job will take me eighteen months."

"That's fine," nodded Odin. "And what about your price?"

The builder looked at the god. "My price is the hand of the goddess Freyja in marriage."

Freyja, sitting among the other goddesses, gasped at the fellow's impudence. "I am *Freyja*," she thought, "most beautiful

of all the goddesses, and this – this *builder* asks *my* hand in marriage? He must be mad!"

The whole assembly seemed to feel as she did. The rafters of Gladsheim rang to shouts of "*No!*" and "*Never!*" and "*Throw the villain out!*" as the furious gods and goddesses shook their fists at the builder.

Odin glowered at him. "What you ask is impossible," he hissed. "Be gone while you still have your life."

The builder was unmoved. "Oh – and I'll also want the sun and the moon," he said. "Freyja, the sun and the moon. That's all."

There was uproar. The builder's life hung in the balance till Loki spoke up. Loki the Sly One he was called, and the Shape-Changer. "Just a minute," he said. "This man's come a long way

to make his offer. We ought not to send him away without at least discussing it. Let him wait outside while we talk."

Reluctantly, the assembly agreed. Freyja was horrified. She hid her face in her hands and wept tears of gold.

"Listen," said Loki. "Why don't we give this fellow six *months* to build the wall?"

"Six months?" the gods laughed. "Impossible!"

Loki nodded, grinning. "Of *course* it's impossible, but a man as vain as this one – a man who thinks he can win the hand of a *goddess* – might well believe he can do it. So, if he agrees, we let him try, and when he fails we send him off empty-handed. That way we've got part of our wall built for nothing. We can't lose."

The Aesir weren't completely happy about Loki's idea, but nobody could say exactly what was wrong with it, and so the builder was allowed back into the hall.

"Six months," Odin told him. "If you can build the wall in six months, the job's yours."

"Six months?" gasped the builder. "You know that's not possible. Nobody could—"

"That's the deal," interrupted Odin. "Take it or leave it."

The builder frowned, deep in thought. After a minute he said, "If I succeed, I get Freyja, the sun and the moon. Is that right?"

Odin nodded. "And if you fail you get nothing. What d'you say?"

"Very well," said the man. "I'll do it."

"There's one rule," said Odin. "Nobody's allowed to help you."

"What about my stallion, Svadilfari? Surely *he* can . . ."

"Nobody!" roared Odin.

Loki looked at him. "Let the stallion help," he urged. "It won't make any difference."

So it was agreed that the stallion might help his master, and before dawn next day, the first day of winter, the work began.

It was a gigantic task. First the builder had to find a hillside from which jutted rocky outcrops and upon whose sides rested giant boulders, half buried, to serve as a quarry. Next he had to start splitting great chunks from the outcrops and digging out the boulders. And when he had some of these materials ready, there was still the problem of moving them to the site of the promised wall. The gods, who had risen early to come out and watch, chuckled among themselves. He'd never do it. Never.

The builder produced a net of stout cords which he spread on the ground. It was huge. As the spectators watched, he began shoving and pushing the chunks of rock he'd freed on to the net. When he had a load, he hitched the stallion to the net and cried, "Walk on, Svadilfari!" The mighty stallion heaved and strained, and slowly the net with its tremendous load was dragged across the ground.

The onlookers were impressed but not worried. "This is only the first load," they told themselves. "The builder will need a thousand such loads to make the wall. His stallion will die of exhaustion long before he can get them, and so will he, the foolish fellow."

Winter came. Day after day, howling gales drove rain, sleet

and snow across the land, but the builder and his horse bowed their heads and gritted their teeth and worked doggedly on. Slowly, slowly the wall grew, following the line of the old wall. As winter gave way to spring, the gods and goddesses became nervous. "Look," they murmured, gazing at the sweating man and his lathered steed. "Nothing stops them. *Nothing*."

The wall had to be finished by the first day of summer if the builder was to claim his payment. With three days to go, only the gateway remained to be built. Freyja broke down and wept. She could see that the builder was going to succeed. So could Odin and the Aesir. Furious with Loki, they assembled to condemn him.

"Who got us into this mess?" they cried. "Whose idea was it?"

Loki looked at them. "It was my idea," he admitted, "but you all agreed."

"You tricked us, that's why!" bellowed Odin. "As you trick everybody. And now this builder's going to succeed and poor Freyja will have to marry him. What can we *do*?"

Loki gazed at Odin. "I swear," he said, "that the builder will never complete his task. You must be calm, and trust me." He strode from the hall.

That night, the builder led Svadilfari down to the quarry as usual. He carried the great net rolled under his arm and he whistled a lively tune as he strode at the horse's side. "Three days," he thought, "and only the gateway to build. Easy." But as they approached the quarry there came a drumming of hoofs and a beautiful mare burst from a stand of trees. She had a glossy coat, a fine silky mane and the largest, softest eyes Svadilfari had ever seen. Enchanted, the stallion broke away from his master and galloped off in pursuit of the mare.

The builder cursed and swore and shouted, but Svadilfari was far away, gambolling with his mate beneath the moon. It was morning by the time he returned, and the builder knew it was too late. The gateway could not be built in time. Filled with

rage, he burst out of his disguise and the gods saw him for what he really was: not a man, but a rock giant.

"We made a bargain with a *man*," they cried, "not a giant. Kill him!"

At this, Thor stepped forward swinging his hammer. A single mighty blow shattered the giant's skull, consigning him to Niflheim for ever. Freyja wept again, this time with joy.

Some time later Loki reappeared in Asgard, leading a colt. It was a strange beast because it had eight legs. Odin was filled with admiration for the colt, so Loki presented it to him. "His name's Sleipnir," he said, "and he's the fastest horse ever seen."

"Where did you find him?" asked Odin, but Loki the Shape-Changer winked and smiled and said nothing.

MONSTROUS CHILDREN
How the gods steal Loki's children

LOKI'S wife was called Sigyn. She was faithful to him and nice enough in her way, but Loki sometimes got restless. Fancied a change. He had a girlfriend in Jotunheim, land of the giants. She was a giantess and her name was Angrboda. From time to time the Shape-Changer would slip away and spend a few days with her. And a few nights. In fact Loki and Angrboda had three children together, and they were all monsters. The eldest was a wolf named Fenrir, the middle child was a great serpent called Jormungand and the youngest was a girl. Her name was Hel and the top half of her was fine. It was the part below the waist which spoiled her, because here the skin was green and black and rotten-looking, and she seemed never to smile. In short, Hel was *not* the sort of girl young men queue up to cuddle.

When the gods got to hear about these children, they were worried. Gods and giants don't mix, so a creature which is half god and half giant is certain to spell trouble sooner or later. They consulted the three Norns.

"They have an evil mother," said Fate.

"Their father is worse," cried Being.

"You can expect only trouble from them," confirmed Necessity.

In the light of this gloomy advice, the gods decided to snatch Loki's children and deal with them once and for all. Odin picked a squad of gods to pull off the snatch, and that night they slipped into Jotunheim. They located Angrboda's hall and burst in upon the sleeping giantess, gagging and tying her before she knew what was happening. Then they grabbed the three monstrous children and dragged them back to Asgard, where Odin was waiting.

He disposed of the serpent first, seizing Jormungand and

hurling him into the sea that surrounded Midgard. The serpent sank to the bottom of the ocean, but he didn't drown. He lived there on the sea bed, growing so long that eventually his great body encircled Midgard till he lay with his tail in his jaws, and he became known as the Midgard Serpent.

Hel was next. Odin lifted the hideous girl above his head and heaved her out of Asgard into the icy blackness of Niflheim, calling after her as she fell, "You will look after the dead, and share your food with them!"

Hel did as Odin had commanded, building for herself in Niflheim a great estate which she shared with the dead. She shared her food with them too, cutting it with a knife called Famine and eating from a plate whose name was Hunger.

Of Loki's monstrous children, only the wolf was left. Odin decided to let Fenrir remain in Asgard. He was only a wolf after all. He put his son Tyr in charge of Fenrir. Everybody else stayed well away from the wolf, but the fearless Tyr fed him with great hunks of meat so that he grew. And grew. And grew.

So big did Fenrir become that the gods were worried, and when the three Norns told them the wolf would cause the death of Odin himself, they knew something had to be done. They couldn't slaughter him because it was forbidden to spill evil blood on the sacred ground of Asgard, so they settled on the next best thing: they'd bind Fenrir so securely he'd pose no threat.

They made a chain of iron links. It was immensely strong – the sort of chain only gods can forge. When it was done they showed it to the wolf.

"Are you as strong as this chain?" they asked.

Fenrir examined the chain. "It's pretty strong," he said, "but I'm stronger."

He did not resist as the gods wound the chain round and round his powerful body. When they'd finished, he planted his paws on the earth, took a deep breath, bunched his muscles and sent broken links pinging in every direction.

The gods were seriously worried now. They hurried away and forged another chain, twice as strong as the first one. So thick and heavy was this chain that a gang of men couldn't even move it. When it was done they showed it to Fenrir. "If you can get out of this," they said, "you'll be famous all over the world for your strength."

Fenrir's grin had fangs in it. "Famous, you say? All over the world? Come on then – tie me up. Nobody ever won fame without taking a chance."

So the gods passed the mighty chain between the wolf's limbs and wound it round and round his body and fastened it at his powerful neck.

"Is that it?" growled the wolf, and he began to buck and kick and writhe and reel and wriggle. He rolled over and over on the ground, hurled himself full tilt against rocks and strained till the muscles bulged beneath his shaggy coat. And just as the gods were beginning to think they had him, the chain burst asunder. Twisted bits of torn iron whined through the air, forcing the gods to throw themselves flat. Fenrir grinned and licked his chops and loped away. "Nobody binds *me*," he thought. "Nobody."

The gods looked at Odin. Odin thought for a while, then said, "*I* know who can make a chain that'll hold him."

"Who?" asked the anxious gods.

"The dwarfs," said Odin, and he sent for Freyr's messenger, whose name was Skirnir.

Skirnir crossed the rainbow bridge into Midgard, then went deep underground to the caves and grottoes where the dwarfs lived. He told them what was required and promised them gold if they succeeded. Dwarfs are extremely fond of gold. They set to work, and before long Skirnir was back in Asgard with the fetter they had made.

Odin peered at it. It looked more like a silken ribbon than a chain. He ran his finger along it. "What's it made of?" he asked.

"Six things," said Skirnir. "The noise of a cat's footsteps. The roots of a mountain. The sinews of a bear. A woman's beard, the breath of a fish and the spit of a bird."

"A cat's footsteps are silent," said Odin, "a woman has no beard, and whoever heard of a mountain with roots?"

"Ah!" smiled Skirnir, "but that's the whole *point*. The *dwarfs* have all the cats' footsteps – that's why we never hear them.

They've got every hair of every woman's beard too, and the breath of all the fishes. Just because *we* don't see these things doesn't mean they don't exist."

The gods weren't all that impressed with the dwarfs' fetter, but they invited Fenrir to go with them to an island in the middle of a lake, and there they showed him the silky cord. "Come on," they challenged, "test your strength against this."

Fenrir looked at the fetter. "Hmmm," he said. "Doesn't *look* much, but you wouldn't have bothered bringing it here unless there was something special about it." He grinned slyly. "I suspect there's magic woven into it, but anyway I wouldn't win much fame breaking a poor-looking thing like this, so you can keep it. *I'll* not let myself be tied with it."

"Oh, come on," urged Odin. "You've smashed iron chains. This'll be *nothing* to you, and anyway, if you can't break it I promise we'll take it off."

The wolf considered this. "Tell you what," he growled softly. "I'll let you tie me up if one of you keeps his hand in my mouth the whole time."

The gods didn't know what to say. They glanced at one another then stared at the ground, shuffling and clearing their throats. Their cheeks were red. Everybody was waiting for somebody else to volunteer. Fenrir watched them, grinning. Finally Tyr stepped forward and placed his hand between the wolf's slavering jaws.

Much relieved, the other gods grabbed the fetter and wound it round Fenrir's body, legs and neck. When they'd finished, the wolf began to thrash about, snarling and flexing his muscles, but he'd been right about the magic. The more he struggled, the

tighter grew the fetter. His struggles became wilder, more frantic. Poor Tyr was jerked and flung about so that his arm was almost wrenched from its socket. The pain was so dreadful that the brave god screamed and yelled, but the wolf kept his fangs firmly clamped on the torn and bleeding hand and when it became clear that he'd never break the fetter, and when he realised the gods didn't mean to untie him, he bit it off.

The rest of the gods were jubilant. It wasn't *their* hand. They fastened a chain to the dwarfs' fetter and passed it through a hole in a gigantic boulder. This boulder they sank a mile into the earth, with another even bigger on top of it to keep it down. Fenrir's jaws gaped and snapped. He howled and slavered. One of the gods drew his sword and jammed it like a prop inside that terrible mouth so that Fenrir was totally helpless.

And that is how they dealt with Loki's brood. None of the three is dead: they are waiting, that's all. The Midgard Serpent lies coiled about the earth, sucking on his tail, Hel sits in Niflheim surrounded by the dead, and Fenrir is bound to his boulder. And there they'll remain. Till Ragnarok.

A FEARSOME BRIDE

Thor and the frost giants

IF the giants of Jotunheim had dared, they would have stormed Asgard, slaughtered the gods and taken the place for themselves. A number of things discouraged them from attempting this, including the mighty wall which surrounded the realm. But what they feared most was Thor's hammer. Thor, the Thunderer, called his hammer Mjolnir, and it had smashed more skulls in its time than all the other hammers in the world put together. Every inhabitant of Asgard knew the importance of Thor's hammer in keeping them safe.

Imagine the consternation, then, when one morning the Thunderer woke to find his hammer gone. Thor raged and bellowed and flung things around as he searched for Mjolnir, but it was no use – the weapon had disappeared.

Now Loki heard Thor crashing about and hurried to see what was wrong. Thor told him and the Shape-Changer said, "Calm down. Don't worry. I'll find Mjolnir for you."

He hurried to the hall of Freyja, the beautiful goddess. "Someone has stolen Thor's hammer," he told her. "Will you lend me your falcon skin so I can search for it?"

Freyja agreed at once. "If my falcon skin were made of pure gold I'd *still* lend it for this great purpose," she said.

So Loki put on the falcon skin and soared into the blue, skimming away over hill and valley till he saw below him Jotunheim, realm of the giants. There on a grassy mound sat Thrym, king of the frost giants. Loki spiralled down and landed beside him.

"Good day," said Thrym. "What are you doing in *Jotunheim* of all places, and how are things in Asgard?"

"Things are not so good in Asgard," said Loki gruffly. "Someone has stolen Thor's hammer. It wasn't *you* by any chance, was it?"

Thrym chuckled hoarsely. "It certainly was," he said. "*I've* got Mjolnir, and I'm hanging on to it till Freyja comes to Jotunheim and marries me."

"Freyja?" gasped Loki. "Marry *you*? Never!"

The frost giant laughed, and his laughter had ice in it. "Then Thor has seen the last of his precious hammer," he said.

Loki knew there was no use in arguing with Thrym. He spread his falcon's wings and launched himself into the wild sky, where he rode the wind all the way home to Asgard.

"Well?" rumbled Thor impatiently as Loki alighted in the courtyard of his hall. "What have you found out, if anything?"

The Sly One pulled a face. "Nothing good, Thunderer. Thrym has your hammer, and he won't return it till we take Freyja to Jotunheim to be his bride."

Loki and Thor hurried to Freyja's hall and told the goddess she must prepare to marry the king of the frost giants.

"*What?*" cried Freyja so loudly that the rafters shook under her lofty roof. So furious was she that her necklace burst apart, scattering gemstones across the floor. "Get out of my hall!" she shrilled. "The pair of you!"

In the face of that awesome rage, the two gods withdrew.

A short time later, all the gods and goddesses met in the great hall Gladsheim to look for a way of getting Mjolnir back.

Heimdall the watchman had a suggestion. "What if –" he glanced at Thor with a twinkle in his eye – "what if we were to dress Thor in a wedding gown and a bridal veil . . ."

His voice was drowned out as the gods and goddesses exploded into laughter. Thor blushed, looking down and muttering to himself.

Heimdall waited for silence, then continued. "We could repair Freyja's necklace and hang it round his snowy, swanlike neck."

More laughter. Thor glowered at the watchman but Heimdall ploughed on, enjoying himself. "We must make him *really* beautiful, a bunch of keys at his slender waist and a long, long dress with brooches at the breast . . ."

The gods and goddesses revelled in Thor's embarrassment. They recognised the excellence of the watchman's plan.

"And we mustn't forget the headdress," concluded Heimdall. "A dainty headdress will set off the rest of her outfit."

Thor, who had always prided himself on his huskiness, was mortified, but the assembly insisted on adopting Heimdall's plan, and so the Thunderer permitted himself to be decked out in the prettiest bridal finery that could be found. Loki put on a woman's clothing too – he would go with the bride to Jotunheim as her maidservant.

In far-off Jotunheim, Thrym's excitement knew no bounds. "She's coming!" he cried. "Freyja the beautiful is on her way to Jotenheim to be my bride. We must *prepare*."

At his command, the hall was decked with swags and garlands of wildflowers. Fresh sweet straw was strewn on the floor. Tables and benches were set out. In the kitchens, cooks and scullions toiled to prepare a rich banquet.

It was evening when the bride and her maidservant arrived. They were welcomed with great ceremony. Servants carried in huge dishes heaped with fine foods from every corner of the world, and set them on the tables with fragrant loaves and flagons of wine. Thrym ushered his bride to the place of honour, bade her be seated and settled himself next to her. The maidservant sat on the giant's other side, and the feasting commenced.

It had been a long journey and Thor was famished.
He ate a whole ox, with eight salmon to follow. After
that he grabbed everything he could reach, cramming
his mouth and scoffing prodigiously, washing the food
down with three horns of mead.

Thrym watched in amazement and delight. "What
an appetite!" he growled. "What a woman!" Unable to
wait any longer he lifted a corner of his bride's veil,
intent on kissing her. But when he saw her eyes he
dropped the gauzy fabric with a cry. "Her eyes!
They burn like fire."

44

The maidservant leaned forward and whispered in his ear, "Freyja was so thrilled by the prospect of marrying you, she hasn't slept for eight nights."

The giant smiled. "Then we'd better let the marriage begin."

"Sire," replied the maid, "I hesitate to mention it at this time, but there's the matter of the hammer . . ."

"Ah – of course." Thrym clapped his hands and bellowed, "The hammer! Bring forth the hammer!"

There was a hurrying and a scurrying and Mjolnir was fetched. The instant he saw it, Thor's heart soared. He leapt to his feet, grabbed the hammer and ripped off his veil. Thrym's pretty bride vanished. Gasps of dismay broke from the assembled giants as they recognised Thor, son of Odin. With a foul oath, Thrym leapt out of his seat but he wasn't fast enough. Thor brought the mighty hammer down on the giant's head, smashing his skull. Thrym's sister was next, and after her died every giant and giantess in the hall. Thor and Loki strode through the carnage and, without a backward glance, mounted their horses and galloped in triumph with the hammer back to Asgard.

RED GOLD
The curse of the dwarf's gold

THE long winter was melting into spring and Odin, Loki and lanky Honir were anxious to be off exploring. One morning, bright and early, the three gods hiked across the rainbow bridge to Midgard. Honir's stride was so long the other two had almost to trot to keep up with him, but the weather was still a bit chilly and their cracking pace kept them warm.

They found a river and decided to walk upstream. They covered many leagues and, late in the afternoon, came to a waterfall. They were hot and hungry, so to cool down they walked through the smoke that thundered and under a curtain of hurtling water that sparkled in the sun. They were gazing, dripping and refreshed, into the seething cauldron at the foot of the fall, when Odin spotted an otter on a nearby bank. The animal had caught a salmon and was resting beside its catch with its eyes closed, unaware of the gods' presence.

Odin pointed the otter out to Loki, who picked up a stone, took careful aim and hurled it with all his might. The stone blurred through the air and struck the otter on the head, killing it instantly.

"How about that, then?" crowed the Shape-Changer. "Two meals with one blow." He waded across and retrieved the otter and the salmon. The water had cooled the trio: the meat and fish would take care of their hunger when they stopped for the night.

They left the waterfall and continued up the valley. It was dusk when they saw a farmhouse ahead and smoke coiling from its chimney. They approached the house and Odin knocked on the door. It was opened by the farmer, whose name was Hreidmar.

"Any chance of a bed for the night?" asked the one-eyed god.

Hreidmar peered at the trio. "*Three* of you?"

"Yes, but we can pay you in food."

"How much food? Enough for my sons? My daughters?"

"Oh, plenty. Show him, Loki."

Loki held up the otter and the salmon. At the sight of the otter the farmer seemed to flinch, but he stepped aside and indicated they should enter. As soon as the three were inside, Hreidmar turned and walked out of the room.

"What's eating him?" asked Loki.

Odin shrugged. "Who cares? We've a roof over our heads and that's all that matters."

"I'm not so sure about that," murmured Honir, to nobody's surprise. Honir was famous for never being sure about anything.

Hreidmar had gone to speak with his sons, Fafnir and Regin. "Your brother's dead," he said.

"Who – Otter?" asked Fafnir. "How d'you know?"

"I've just been shown his body," grated Hreidmar, "by those who murdered him. They're staying the night here."

Filled with rage, Fafnir and Regin swore to avenge their brother, Otter.

"There are three of 'em," warned Hreidmar.

"There are three of us," retorted Fafnir.

"Aye," the farmer, who was also a weaver of spells, nodded. "At my signal we'll tackle one each, and I'll see if I can't magic 'em out of some of their powers."

Hreidmar and his two remaining sons entered the room where the gods sat waiting, and as they began to converse, the farmer gave the signal and the three of them leapt on Odin, Loki and Honir. Thanks to Hreidmar's magic, Odin lost his grip on his spear and Loki's sky shoes fell off his feet. After a brief struggle the three gods found themselves lying bound on the floor. Hreidmar, panting, glared down on them. "Otter was my son," he hissed, "and you killed him. Now I shall kill the three of you."

"But he was just an *otter*," protested Odin.

"By *day* he took the form of an otter," snarled Fafnir, "the better to catch the fish we need to eat. By night he was a man, and our brother."

"I wouldn't have killed him if I'd known that," said Loki, "but how was I to know?"

"Listen, Hreidmar," interrupted Odin. "It's obvious we didn't mean to kill your son. What if we pay you a *ransom* for his life? You can name the amount and we'll get it."

The farmer gazed at Odin. "Will you swear an oath on that? I get whatever ransom I demand, or the three of you die?"

"Certainly," said Odin.

"Very well." Hreidmar turned to Fafnir. "Take Otter's body to your sisters. Tell them to skin him and bring the pelt to me."

When the pelt came, Hreidmar showed it to his captives. "Right. I want this pelt crammed with red gold, and when it's full I want it covered with a heap of red gold, so no part of it can be seen."

"Agreed," said Odin.

He turned and murmured some instructions to Loki. Loki nodded, then looked at the farmer. "Untie me," he said. "I'll fetch the gold while you hold my two friends hostage."

Loki was freed. He strode to the door, chuckling at some private joke, and vanished in the night.

Loki travelled across Midgard, none too swiftly because his sky shoes were back at Hreidmar's place. Reaching the island of Hlesey, he visited Aegir the sea god and his wife Ran in their hall on the sea bed. There he borrowed Ran's drowning net and journeyed on till he reached a hole in the ground. He wriggled through this hole and went down, down, down, till he came to a great echoing cavern with a pool of black water. In the water lay a gigantic pike. Loki cast Ran's net into the water and hauled out the snapping, wriggling pike. He grabbed the pike, shook it and hissed, "Change shape!"

At once the fish vanished and Loki found himself holding the dwarf Andvari.

"Whaddya want?" screeched the dwarf.

"All your red gold," snarled Loki, "or I'll break every bone in your ugly little body."

"All right, all right," whined the dwarf. "Follow me."

He led the god to the forge where he turned gold into beautiful objects. There were bars and coins and scraps and splashes of red gold everywhere.

"Sweep it all up," snapped Loki. "Put it in these two sacks. And get a move on."

The dwarf was far from happy, but he daren't argue. Soon the forge was empty of gold, while the two sacks were full. Loki took a last look around to make sure, and his sharp eyes caught a glint on Andvari's finger. "What about that?" he growled, pointing to the ring.

"It's just a ring," whimpered the dwarf. "A small ring. Let me keep it, please."

"Hand it over," grated Loki. "Now."

Reluctantly, Andvari took off the ring and gave it to Loki, who slipped it on his own finger. As Loki hefted the two sacks, the dwarf hissed, "I curse that ring and all my gold. Whoever comes to own it will be destroyed."

"Good," grinned Loki, thinking of Hreidmar and his sons.

"Nobody robs me and gets away with it!" screeched the dwarf.

"Splendid," smiled Loki. "I'll be sure and pass on your kind words." He threw a sack of gold over each shoulder and strode away through the network of caverns.

"At last," growled Odin. "I thought you weren't coming back."

Loki grinned. "Would I leave my friends here to die?"

Honir gazed at him. "I don't know," he murmured. "You might."

Hreidmar cut the captives' bonds, hardly able to tear his eyes away from the gold. Otter's pelt was fetched, and filled to bursting with gold from the first sack. Then it was laid on the floor, and the second sack was emptied over it. Hreidmar examined the glittering heap minutely. "This won't do!" he cried. "I can see a whisker. The deal's off. You're all going to die."

"Just a minute." Loki twisted Andvari's ring from his finger. "Here – this'll hide the whisker."

While Hreidmar and his sons gloated over the gold, Odin retrieved his great spear and Loki put on his sky shoes. Thus fortified, the three gods strode out of the house.

In the doorway Loki turned and said, "Oh – by the way. The ring and all that gold belong to the dwarf Andvari. He put a curse on it. His exact words were: *Whoever comes to own it will be destroyed.* I just thought I'd tell you."

Hreidmar's cheeks paled and he glanced fearfully at the gold. When he looked up, Loki had gone. There was just his mocking laughter in the wind.

AN APPLE A DAY

How Idun is rescued from the giants

ON a morning of sun and wind and scudding cloud, Odin, Loki and Honir crossed the flaming rainbow bridge to continue their exploration of Midgard. They strode out over hill and gully, moor and meadow, talking and laughing. So content were they to be together on such a day that their minds never turned to thoughts of food till they had covered many a league and the sun's rim was on the horizon. "Hey," said Odin then, "my belly thinks my throat's been cut. Which of you's got the grub?"

"I haven't," said Loki.

"Me neither," said Honir. "I don't think food was mentioned, was it – when we were making arrangements, I mean?"

"Dunno," growled Odin. "All I know is . . ."

"Look." Loki pointed. "On that hillside, a herd of oxen. All we have to do is pick out a fine fat beast and do it in, and there's supper."

"Oooh." Honir looked doubtful. "Do you think we *should?* I mean, they probably *belong* to somebody."

"Why don't you shut up, Daddy-long-legs?" rumbled Odin rudely.

So the three gods singled out a fine ox and killed it. They cut the meat into great joints, lit a fire and put the meat in the flames to roast. They were so hungry that the smell of cooking made them slaver.

"Give it a poke," said Odin after a while. "It'll be about ready, I reckon."

But when Loki jabbed the meat with his dagger, blood trickled out. He shook his head. "Not yet."

They sat gazing into the fire. Their stomachs rumbled so loudly it was like thunder. Presently Honir said, "I'm not absolutely sure, but I think perhaps . . ."

Loki jabbed the meat again, and another trickle of blood hissed and bubbled on the coals. "Raw," he muttered, "as the minute we started roasting it."

"But surely that's *impossible?*" cried Honir.

Odin shook his head. "It's some sort of magic. Somebody's playing a trick on us."

"Somebody certainly is," said a voice above their heads. "Look up."

They were sitting under a great oak, and when they looked up there was an eagle gazing down at them.

"Let me have my pick of the meat," said the eagle, "and your supper will cook perfectly."

The three discussed this for a moment, then Odin nodded. "All right," he said. "We agree. We've got to, or we'll starve to death."

The eagle spread its wings, flapped down to the fireside and began pulling hunks of meat from the flames. It took both shoulders and the rump.

"Hey!" cried Odin. "We didn't say you could take all the best bits."

The bird ignored him, dragging the meat to a convenient stump and tearing at it with its great hooked beak.

Loki was so angry that he leapt up, raised his staff and rammed it into the eagle's body. There was a thud and a puff of feathers. The eagle let out a shrill cry and launched itself into flight, trailing the staff. To his horror Loki found he couldn't let go his end, and as the mighty bird flapped away he was dragged, bumping and scraping, over the rough ground. The eagle made no attempt to go higher but skimmed the earth, and within seconds Loki's legs and body were bruised, skinned and bleeding. "Stop!" he screamed, writhing and kicking on the end of the trailing staff. "Let me down!"

"I'll let you down on one condition," said the eagle.

"Anything!" cried Loki.

"I want the goddess Idun and her basket of apples. You must swear to lure her out of Asgard so that I can grab her."

Loki said nothing. It had dawned on him that this eagle must be a giant in disguise. Whatever happened, he mustn't swear to do as his tormentor wished. Loki's silence enraged the eagle. It swooped, dashing Loki against a rocky outcrop, dragging him through a stand of thistles and bumping his raw kneecaps on a fallen tree.

"Very well!" screeched poor Loki, who could stand the pain no longer. "I swear."

At once he was able to relax his grip on the staff. He fell on springy turf, rolling over and over. The eagle shook out the staff and soared away. Loki picked himself up and dragged his battered body back the way he'd come.

Seven days passed, and then Loki the trickster approached Idun as she strolled with her basket of apples through a meadow in Asgard.

"Idun," he said, "I have seen such a sight in Midgard as you would not believe."

Idun smiled her innocent smile. "Oh – and what sight might that be, Loki?"

"An apple tree," lied Loki, "with golden apples twice as beautiful as any I've seen in your basket."

Idun gazed at him. "But surely that's not possible, since my apples bestow unending youth?"

Loki shrugged. "Perhaps the apples I saw also prevent ageing. Anyway, I think you should come with me and see."

Now everybody knew that Loki was a trickster, but Idun was innocent and didn't stop to think. Over the rainbow bridge she

trotted at Loki's heels, anxious to view the wondrous apples. The eagle, who was really a giant called Thiassi, was waiting. The minute Idun set foot in Midgard he swooped, grabbed her with his horny talons and bore her and her basket of apples away to Jotunheim. There he imprisoned her in his stronghold, Thrymheim. "Now," he cried, "the gods and goddesses will grow old and die, but I shall live for ever!"

The situation in Asgard soon became grim. Without Idun's apples, the gods and goddesses began to age. Their beauty faded. They hobbled about in lumpy old clothes and thick stockings, holding their backs and groaning. Their hair was grey and their conversation was about illness and varicose veins and how food didn't taste like it used to, and the terrible things young people got up to these days.

Odin kept meaning to call an emergency meeting but his arthritis was killing him and it slipped his mind. When he finally got round to it everybody came except Loki and, of course, Idun. "We *must* find Idun," he croaked, fiddling with a loose thread on his fawn cardigan. "Has anybody seen her lately?"

"I saw her crossing Bifrost with Loki," said Heimdall.

The gods and goddesses looked at one another. Odin sighed. "That probably explains why she's missing. Bring him in, will you?"

They had to search for the trickster but they found him eventually, dozing in Idun's field. They seized him, tied him up and dragged him to Gladsheim. Odin glowered at him. "We know you lured Idun away," he growled. "And if you don't bring her back, you're dead."

"If he doesn't bring her back we're *all* dead," grunted Heimdall.

"I lured Idun away," admitted Loki, "but I had no choice."

He told the geriatric assembly about the eagle who was really the giant Thiassi. When he'd finished Odin said, "That's *your* problem, Loki. You took her, you get her back. Otherwise we kill you."

Loki stared at the decrepit but implacable god. "Not much of a choice, is it?" He nodded. "All right I'll try, if Freyja will lend me her falcon skin."

Freyja, beautiful no longer, gladly lent the skin, and Loki flew to Jotunheim and to the mountain stronghold of Thrymheim. It was a case of lucky Loki, because Thiassi had gone fishing with his daughter. Loki found Idun imprisoned in a small room. Swiftly the trickster cast a spell which turned the goddess into a nut. Seizing the nut with his falcon's claws, Loki launched himself into the sky and flew as fast as he could towards Asgard.

It was only minutes later that the giant and his daughter arrived home. Finding his captive fled, Thiassi turned himself once more into an eagle and soared skyward in pursuit of the falcon. He was much larger than Loki, with far more powerful wings. The distance between the two birds shortened. Seeing the eagle gaining on him Loki beat his wings desperately, straining every sinew to reach the walls round Asgard. Odin, from his high seat, saw the falcon approaching, and the great eagle which pursued it. At once he ordered a great heap of kindling to be piled against the wall. Gods stood poised with burning brands to light the fire at his signal. Loki saw these preparations from afar and dived towards that section of wall.

The eagle was so close now he could hear the whistle of air through its pinions. With the last of his strength Loki swooped low over the wall, hurtling like a thunderbolt into Asgard. Odin at once gave the signal. The gods plunged their torches into the great drift of kindling. Flames roared skyward. The eagle, unable to swerve, flew straight into them. Its wing feathers caught fire and it fell like a meteor, trailing smoke. As it hit the ground some gods and goddesses ran with spears to finish it off. The giant Thiassi was dead.

Loki, who had resumed his real shape, mumbled some magic words and the nut became Idun again. The wrinkled inhabitants of Asgard came creaking and hobbling from all directions. Idun smiled, handing out apples. Gods and goddesses bit into them. The air was filled with the sound of crunching.

A MISTLETOE WAND

Balder the beautiful god

BALDER, son of Odin and Frigg, was the most beautiful of all the gods and everybody loved him. They loved him for his golden hair, his glowing complexion and, most of all, for his sweet disposition. Surrounded by all this admiration, Balder *ought* to have been happy, but he was not, because his nights were plagued by dreams so hideous that he dreaded sleep. His dreams were of dark, formless beings which surrounded him in a place of shadows, cold beyond imagining. He believed the dreams foreshadowed his death.

The gods and goddesses gathered to discuss the meaning of Balder's nightmares. Why, they wondered, should such fearsome spectres haunt a man as kind and gentle as their beloved Balder? They talked and talked, but nobody could fathom the meaning of the dreams. Presently Odin said, "Enough of this, I will go to Niflheim and seek an explanation there."

Odin mounted eight-legged Sleipnir and rode till he reached the hall of Hel, keeper of the dead. Striding in, he was amazed to see the place decked out as though for a celebration. He was gazing about him when Hel herself appeared. Her face and body were those of a living woman, but her thighs, legs and

feet were those of a rotting corpse. Odin looked at her. "Why is your hall decked out like this? Are you expecting somebody important?"

Hel nodded. "I expect Balder," she said.

"But Balder is both beautiful and popular," said Odin. "Why should he die? Who would want to harm him?"

"Balder will die at the hands of his blind brother Hodr," said Hel.

This seemed impossible to Odin, but Hel would say no more, so he mounted Sleipnir and rode back to Asgard with a heavy heart.

When they heard Odin's news, the gods and goddesses were distraught. They began listing the ways a man might die – by water, fire, iron, stone and so forth. There *must* be a way to protect Balder from *every* sort of death, if only they could think how to go about it.

Frigg, Balder's mother, said, "*I* know. I'll make *everything* on earth swear an oath not to harm my son. I'll go to iron, fire, water and stone. I'll go to wood and bone, famine and disease. By the time I've finished, there'll be nothing on earth that can hurt Balder."

So off went Frigg, and nothing could resist her sweet petitioning. Every creature in the world, and every substance, and every sort of disease swore a solemn oath never to harm Balder. The goddess returned to Asgard well pleased, and when she told the gods and goddesses, they were much relieved.

Balder felt a lot better too. In fact he felt so great he invented a game. In this game he would stand perfectly still while the inhabitants of Asgard took turns chucking an assortment of missiles at him: stones, sticks, lumps of iron, the odd dwarf – it didn't matter what. Everything simply bounced off without harming him. He didn't feel a thing.

One day, Loki passed by as a game of bounce stuff off Balder was in progress. He stopped to watch. Everybody seemed to be having a great time, laughing and falling about. Now Loki wasn't keen on happiness. Strife and suffering were more in his line. He watched for a while, and as he watched an idea came to him. He went off and found a quiet spot, and there he changed his shape.

Loki was now a smelly old woman with a hairy top lip. Thus disguised, he hobbled off to Frigg's hall. The goddess was none too pleased when this ragged crone shuffled in, but she was too polite to kick her out. "What do you want, old woman?" she asked.

"I want nothing," Loki replied. "I came from Midgard to see the wonders of Asgard, but all I've seen so far is a gang of gods pelting some poor young man with stones. Killing him, they were. I didn't expect to see stuff like that in the realm of the gods."

Frigg chuckled. "They weren't killing him, old woman. He's my son, and nothing on earth can hurt him. What you saw is just a game they play."

The crone's toothless mouth fell open. "You say *nothing* can hurt him? Nothing at all?"

"Not a thing."

"What if a mountain fell on his head?"

"It wouldn't harm him."

"Well – suppose someone swiped his head off with a really keen sword?"

"They couldn't – the sword would just bounce off."

"You don't say." The old woman shook her head. "That's powerful magic. Who *did* that?"

"I did," boasted Frigg. "I travelled to every corner of the nine worlds and everything swore an oath never to hurt Balder."

"*Everything?* Every single thing? Are you absolutely sure?"

"Well . . ." Frigg smiled. "There *is* one small mistletoe plant in Valhalla. I didn't bother asking *it* to swear – it's too frail to harm anyone."

"Hmmmmm." The old woman treated the goddess to a toothless smile. "Well, thank you for putting up with a nosy old woman. I'll be off now."

"Goodbye then," said Frigg. "Enjoy the rest of your visit."

As soon as he was alone, Loki resumed his own shape and hurried off to Valhalla to look for the mistletoe plant. He found it growing on an oak tree as mistletoe does, and wrenched it free. Examining the plant, he saw that one of its twigs was dead straight and fairly thick. It was about as long as his forearm. He tore this twig loose and threw away the rest of the plant. Then he set off towards the great hall, Gladsheim, where he'd seen the game in progress.

It was still on when Loki got there. On the way, he'd whittled one end of the mistletoe wand to a sharp point. He sidled up and joined the happy spectators.

Looking around, Loki spotted Balder's blind brother, Hodr, standing off to one side. He worked his way over, poked the lad in the ribs and cried, "Now then, Hodr!" so loudly that Hodr jumped.

"Oh!" he cried. "It's Loki, isn't it?"

"Sure is," chuckled the trickster. "Listen, why aren't you joining in the fun?"

Hodr shrugged. "How *can* I? I can't *see* my brother, let alone throw things at him. And anyway I've nothing to throw."

"You could throw this," murmured Loki, placing the mistletoe wand in the blind god's hands. "It's just a twig, but at least you'll have had a go."

"But – how am I to know where?"

"I'll stand behind you and guide your aim," said Loki. "Come on."

He led Hodr forward. They had to wait, because gods were lining up to hurl things at Balder. Gradually they shuffled forward till it was their turn. "Now, Hodr," murmured Loki, "your brother's in front of you and a touch to the left, about fifteen paces away. Raise the wand like a dart. That's it. Now, if I turn you just a fraction, like this – that's it. Now. Throw!"

Hodr's arm was strong. Loki's aim was true. The wand whistled through the air, struck Balder in the middle of his chest and passed clean through him. For a moment Balder continued to stand. There was a startled look on his face. Then, without uttering a sound, he pitched forward and fell dead to the ground.

The spectators stood dumbfounded. The participants gaped. Nobody spoke. Hodr, sensing something wrong, turned his head from side to side. "Wh – what is it?" he stammered. "What's happening?"

He felt behind him for Loki, but Loki had gone.

THOKK

Loki tricks the gods

SUCH a weeping and a wailing in Asgard now. Balder dead. Loki fled. Bitter tears in Gladsheim shed.

A Viking's funeral. They bore Balder's poor pierced body down to the sea and laid it in his longship, *Ringhorn*. His wife, Nanna, was so filled with grief that her heart broke and she died, and so they laid her at her husband's side. Then they heaped the ship with arms and with treasures and all the things the couple might need on their last, terrible voyage to the everlasting cold of Niflheim. So heavy was the ship, and so weak the gods from weeping, that they had to enlist the help of the giantess Hyrrokin to launch it.

When it was in the water, Odin clambered aboard and gazed for the last time on the face of his beautiful son. Then he plunged a burning brand into Balder's pyre and leapt ashore. The wind filled the sail and fanned the flames and *Ringhorn* put to sea, trailing smoke. Gods and goddesses, elves and giants watched through their tears as the burning ship, low in the water now, rolled and bobbed out towards the horizon. White vapour rose with the smoke as brine and pyre mingled, and, not long after that, *Ringhorn* vanished for ever beneath the waves.

Frigg couldn't bear her grief. "Will someone – anyone – *please* ride to Niflheim and ask the Keeper of the Dead to let my Balder come home again?" she pleaded.

Nobody spoke. Nobody wanted to brave that awful journey, nor enter Hel's dread realm. Frigg's eyes searched out their faces one by one, and one by one they looked at the ground.

Then brave Hermod, son of Odin and Balder's brother, stepped forward. "I will go," he said.

Odin ordered eight-legged Sleipnir, fastest horse in the nine worlds, to be saddled. Hermod mounted, clapped his spurs to the horse's flank and galloped away.

For nine days he rode northward and downward along a valley which narrowed and grew darker with every league. The strip of sky far above him thinned and thinned, till presently the earth closed over his head and Sleipnir was galloping down, down into the cold dark underworld.

The way stretched on and on. Hermod was beginning to

think he'd somehow missed Hel's domain when it loomed out of the freezing fog before him – a lofty hall, dark and silent. He dismounted, took a deep breath to calm his fear and strode inside. To either side for as far as he could see stood rows and rows of benches, and every bench was crowded with the foul and rotting dead. They uttered no sound but turned to gaze at the newcomer, some through milky eyes, some through sunken eyes and some through empty sockets, but Hermod didn't return their gaze. He'd spotted Balder in the place of honour, though his brother showed no sign of recognition. Of Hel there was no trace, but then it *was* very late: she'd no doubt retired to bed. Anxious to stay as far away from the dead as possible, Hermod settled himself by the door to await whatever travesty of dawn this awful place afforded.

Under the mute gaze of a thousand corpses he dozed and woke, dozed and woke. Hel's rest seemed to be lasting for ever, but presently she appeared, dragging her rotting legs between

the crowded benches. She didn't speak, but stood on the slimy floor, glowering at the intruder. Hermod greeted the hideous creature and said, "I am sent by the gods and goddesses in Asgard to ask that Balder be permitted to return with me to the land of the living."

Slowly, Hel shook her head. "Nobody returns from the place of the dead," she droned. "Nobody."

"Oh, but Balder – Balder was the *light* of Asgard," murmured Hermod. "He was its *joy*, its very *soul*. Without Balder there is no life, no love, no purpose. Please make this *one* exception. We'll never ask again."

Hel looked at Hermod for a long time. Then she said, "I can't believe Balder was that important. People die. Life goes on. Nobody's indispensable."

"Nobody except Balder," said Hermod. "Believe me, without him Asgard's very nearly as dark and as cold – as *this* foul place."

"Hmmm." Hel frowned. "I'll tell you what I'll do. I'll release Balder from death – let him live again – if *everything* in the nine worlds weeps for him. But it has to be *everything*. If one creature, one substance, one anything refuses to weep for Balder, he stays here. Do you agree?"

Hermod chewed his lip, thinking. He'd hoped to take Balder back with him, but clearly it wasn't to be. This was probably the best deal he'd get from the Keeper of the Dead. He nodded. "Very well – I agree. I'll tell them in Asgard."

When Hermod delivered his message a wave of hope surged through the realm of the gods. The appeal went out across the nine worlds for everybody and everything to weep for Balder.

The gods wept, and the goddesses, and the elves and dwarfs and giants. The trees wept, and gold, copper and silver. Water wept, and fire and air and earth and all the diseases. It seemed Balder the beautiful would live again.

Then one of Asgard's messengers found a giantess sitting in a cave. She said her name was Thokk, and that she wouldn't weep for Balder. The messenger begged and pleaded, but the giantess wouldn't budge. "Never liked him," she growled. "Let him rot in Niflheim, that's what *I* say."

So the sad messenger trailed back to Asgard with his news. He expected the gods to rise up in fury and sally forth to make the giantess weep one way or another, but they didn't. They only groaned and shook their grizzled heads and crept away to their halls looking old and weary. And so Balder stayed in Niflheim, thanks to Thokk. Thokk, also known as Shape-Changer, whose real name was Loki.

THE TRICKSTER TRICKED
The gods avenge Balder's death

LOKI was scared. He knew that soon the minds of the gods would turn from thoughts of mourning Balder to thoughts of avenging his death. Hodr had actually flung the fatal wand, but all of Asgard knew that Loki had been behind the murder. He had to get away.

He crossed the rainbow bridge into Midgard and headed for the mountains. There he found a steep valley with a river whose waters ran down to the sea. The head of this valley was a chaos of tumbled boulders, frost-fractured rock and treacherous, sliding scree. By using the materials to hand, the trickster was able to build himself a shelter which merged so perfectly with its background that a stranger passing by would not have known there was a house there at all.

He didn't feel safe though. Never. Indoors he would start up at every little noise. The call of a gull. The skitter of a stone down a scree slope. Out of doors he found himself forever looking over his shoulder or watching the skyline. Deep down he knew the gods would find him someday. It was a matter of clinging on to his freedom as long as possible.

Not far from Loki's hiding place was a mighty waterfall known as Franang's Falls. One day, gazing into the thunderous white water at the base of the fall, Loki had an idea. "Sometimes," he told himself, "I will take the form of a salmon and lie in these seething waters. *Nobody* will find me then." So from time to time Loki the Shape-Changer became a great salmon that lay in the cool green pool beneath the roaring maelstrom, but even here he was never truly at ease.

One day, in his own shape and sitting in his house, Loki heard the sound he had dreaded – the sound of voices. He'd been doodling with some linen threads, knotting them into a fine net. Now he leapt up, flung the net into the fire and hurried out of the house. A group of gods was making its way up the valley. They hadn't spotted the shelter yet, but Loki could tell by the purposeful way they moved that they knew what they were looking for. He had no doubt that Odin had seen the house from his high seat, Hlidskjalf, from which he was able to look out over the nine worlds and with his one eye see everything that went on. He whirled, bounding down the steep slope to the pool below the waterfall. There he took the form of a salmon and plunged into the spume.

The gods spotted the house. First inside was wise Kvasir. He looked all around. Nobody was here, but on the hearth a fire smouldered and in it, reduced to ash, he saw the pattern of a net. He smiled grimly at his companions. "See – a net. Why a net? To catch a fish, perhaps? Come – let *us* make a net."

So they made a net, a stout net, wide enough to stretch across the river, and first thing next morning they took it down to the falls. Thor grabbed one end of the net and waded across the river. Then the gods began a slow trawl downstream. In order to evade the net, Loki was forced to swim before it. He could easily do this while the river was wild and deep, but he knew that at the foot of the valley it became wide, slow and shallow on the last leg of its journey to the sea. If the gods drove him into the shallows he'd be grounded and they'd have him. He found a narrow cleft where the water rushed between two boulders and wedged himself in there till the gods passed by.

The net slid across Loki's slippery back but did not catch him.

When they didn't see his dorsal fin in the shallows, the gods realised that Loki had somehow given them the slip. They returned to the pool under the falls, where they fastened stone weights all along the lower edge of the net. This time it would not be possible for anything to escape by passing under it.

They began a second trawl. This time Loki was really worried. The trick he'd used the first time would be useless now. He swam downstream with the gods and their net on his tail. The shallows weren't far away. He could hear how the waters grew quiet. A stone's throw and he'd be stranded.

There was only one course open to him and that was to turn, rush back towards his pursuers and leap right over the net. He turned and swam upstream, battling the current, building up speed. With the net a hand's-breadth in front of his nose he shot upwards, broke surface and curved through the air in a shower of sparkling droplets. He heard the gods shout, then he was over the net and away upstream, carving the water with powerful sweeps of his tail.

Wearily the gods dragged themselves once more to the head of the valley to begin another trawl. This time Thor stayed in midstream, wading down behind the net, watching the surface beyond it. Again Loki was forced downstream. He knew where Thor was, and why, and as he swam he racked his brain for some new trick. This time his wits deserted him. With the shallows in front and the net close behind, the best he could think to do was leap again.

This time Thor was ready. As the great fish broke surface he opened his arms. Loki flicked his tail hard over, trying for a mid-air swerve but he didn't get it. His leap was carrying him straight at the god's chest. Thor's arms closed like a trap and Loki found himself hanging head downwards, gasping in an iron hug. It was all up with him and he knew it.

To keep from drowning in air, Loki resumed his proper shape. The gods split into two parties: one to wreak vengeance on Shape-Changer, the other to hunt down his sons, Vali and Narvi. When they caught them they turned Vali into a wolf, which leapt on Narvi and tore out his throat before bounding away in the direction of Jotunheim. The gods ripped out Narvi's entrails and carried them to the cave where their companions had taken Loki. There they bound Shape-Changer to three great rocks, using Narvi's entrails as bonds. Flat on his back lay Loki, gazing up at the dripping stalactites that hung from the cave's roof.

His son's innards were like bands of iron round his body, legs and neck. He was totally helpless. And the gods went outside and caught a poisonous snake, which they tied to a stalactite directly over the captive's head. Venom from this snake would have dripped endlessly on to Loki's face, if his faithful wife Sigyn had not chosen to remain with him. She caught most of the venom in a wooden bowl. Only when she was forced to carry the bowl away and empty it did venom splash down on her husband. When this happened he would cry out in torment, struggling uselessly against his bonds. The gods surveyed their handiwork, then turned and departed. Their task was done. Balder was avenged. Loki would lie bound in the depths of that cold wet cave, age upon age, till Ragnarok.

RAGNAROK
The end of the world

ALL things have their beginning, and their end. Even worlds. This is how it will be at Ragnarok, the last battle.

First, war in Midgard. Three years it will rage. Brother will fight brother, fathers will slaughter their sons. There will be no law, but every sort of abomination.

Then, hard on the heels of war, will come three winters so hard as to make past winters seem like summer. Blizzards will howl over Midgard from the four corners of the earth. No summers will divide these three winters. Blackened by frost and choked with snow, the world will sicken towards death, and the time will be called Fimbulvetr.

Worse will follow when Skoll, the wolf who pursues the sun, runs down his prey and swallows it. His brother Hati will catch and rend the moon, and the stars too will vanish from the sky. The world, already drenched with blood, will be steeped in darkness. And the darkness will breed earthquakes, so that trees and mountains fall. Every fetter will be loosed. The wolf Fenrir will run free, and the giants and the dwarfs and the dead. The Midgard Serpent will spit out his tail and thrash the seas into waves as he twists towards dry land. And on those crashing waters a ship will pitch and yaw – a ship made out of dead men's nails and crammed with giants intent on invading Asgard. Loki's bonds will break and he too will sail for the realm of the gods, and in his ship will be all the dead of Niflheim.

Then the wolf Fenrir and Jormungand the Midgard Serpent, who are brothers, will move together across the blasted land. Fenrir's jaws will gape and slaver and Jormungand will spit venom, poisoning the earth. The sky will be torn to shreds as the sons of Muspell, led by the mighty Surt, march north against Asgard. The tramp of their feet over Bifrost will shatter the rainbow bridge behind them, so that the monsters and giants and all of the dead are marooned in Asgard with no way back. And they will gather on the plain of Vigrid, so numerous as to be uncountable.

Summoned by their watchman's blast on the great horn Gjall, the gods will don their armour and grasp their swords and spears. The warriors of Valhalla will join them, and together this mighty army will march towards Vigrid with Odin at their head. On arrival, Odin will charge the wolf Fenrir, while Thor joins battle with the Midgard Serpent. Freyr will challenge Surt, leader of the fire giants of Muspell, who will kill him. One-handed Tyr will die too, his throat ripped out by the hound Garm.

Heimdall, watchman of the gods, will fight Loki, and both will die. The struggle between Thor and Jormungand will be a fierce one. At the end Thor will slay the serpent, but then he too will die, overcome by Jormungand's venom. Odin and Fenrir will fight on till the wolf finds an opening, seizes the Father of the Gods and swallows him. At once Vidar, son of Odin, will plant his foot on Fenrir's lower jaw, pinning it to the ground

before seizing the upper jaw and wrenching it so hard as to rip the wolf apart, thus avenging his father. In his rage, Surt the fire giant will fling flame in every direction. Asgard will catch fire, and Midgard and Jotunheim and Niflheim. All will burn. All creatures – gods and giants, dwarfs and monsters, warriors and women and children and men – will die. The birds will perish, and the animals and fishes. The nine worlds will be utterly consumed. There will be no sun, no moon, no stars. The land will sink beneath the sea. Absolute silence will reign, and utter darkness.

But see! A man and a woman have hidden themselves in the branches of Yggdrasil, the tree that was, and is, and will always be. Their names are Lif and Lifthrasir. When the earth rises once more out of the sea, when there is a new sun, a new moon and a skyful of new stars, these two will leave their hiding place. They will lie together. Sons and daughters will be born to them.

The land will be green and fertile, with corn and fruit and pasture. Creatures will reappear – birds and cows and fishes. Vidar and Vali, sons of Odin, will be there too, having survived Ragnarok. Balder and Hodr and Honir will return from the land of the dead. Gods and goddesses, women and men, dwarfs and giants, plants and creatures will come together to make a new world. For life is like a serpent whose tail is in its mouth: when we come to the end, there is the beginning. And over all endings and all beginnings spread the branches of Yggdrasil, the tree that was, and is, and will always be.

FIMBULVETR (*fim*-bul-vet-ur) Three-year winter before Ragnarok, the end of the world.

FRANANG'S FALLS (*fran*-ang's falls) Waterfall. Loki hid in the pool at its foot, disguised as a salmon.

FREYJA (*frey*-ah) Goddess. Sister of Freyr. She was the most beautiful of the goddesses and many dwarfs and giants wanted her as their bride. This often caused problems for the gods, who didn't want to give her up.

FREYR (*frey*-er) God. Brother of Freyja.

FRIGG (frig) Goddess. Wife of Odin and mother of Balder.

GARM (garm) Hound belonging to Hel who guards the entrance to Niflheim.

GINNUNGAGAP (*gin*-un-ga-gap) Void which separated Muspell from Niflheim before the world began.

GJALL (g-yall) The horn with which Heimdal will summon the Aesir to Ragnarok, the last battle.

GLADSHEIM (*glads*-hime) Great hall in Asgard where the gods and goddesses hold assemblies.

HATI (*hah*-tee) Means 'hated', the name of the wolf who pursues the moon and will swallow it before Ragnarok, the end of the world.

HEIMDAL (*hime*-dall) Watchman of the gods and guardian of Bifrost, the rainbow bridge.

HEL (hell) Daughter of Loki and Keeper of the Dead.

HEL (hell) Realm of the dead. It bears the same name as its ruler.

HERMOD (*hair*-mod) God. Rode to Hel to try to rescue his brother Balder. He was responsible for welcoming dead heroes to Valhalla.

HLESEY (*hless*-ee) An island near where the sea god Aegir and his wife Ran live.

HLIDSKJALF (*hlid*-sk-yalf) Odin's seat in Asgard from which he can see over all the nine worlds.

HODR (*hoe*-dr) Blind god tricked by Loki into striking down Balder.

HONIR (*ho*-near) Lanky god who can never make up his mind.

HREIDMAR (*hride*-mar) Farmer who can work magic. Father of Otter.

HYRROKIN (*hirro*-kin) Friendly giantess, who helps launch Balder's funeral boat, *Ringhorn*.

IDUN (Id-*doon*) Goddess and wife of Bragi. She holds the apples of eternal youth which keep the Aesir young.

JORMUNGAND (*yore*-mun-gand)
Enormous serpent son of Loki and
Angrboda. The Midgard Serpent who lives
in the sea and surrounds Midgard, biting
on his own tail to complete the circle.

JOTUNHEIM (*Yo*-tun-hime)
Realm of giants.

KVASIR (*kvah*-seer) Wise god who helps
catch Loki when he takes the form of a
salmon and hides in the waterfall.

LIF (leaf) Man who will survive
Ragnarok, the end of the world, and
father a new race of humans.

LIFTHRASIR (*Leaf*-thra-seer)
Woman who will survive Ragnarok by
hiding with Lif in Yggdrasil. Mother
of a new race of humans.

LOKI (*lo*-kee) Mischievous god.
Also called Shape-Changer, Sky-Walker,
Trickster and Sly One. The betrayer of
the Aesir.

MIDGARD (*mid*-gard)
The realm of men and women.

MJOLNIR (m-*yoll*-near) Thor's hammer.
It was forged by dwarfs.

MUNDILFARI (*moon*-dill-farri)
A man, father of Moon and Sun.

MUSPELL (*muss*-pell) Realm of fire,
ruled by Surtr.

NANNA (*nan*-ah) Wife of Balder.

NARVI (*nar*-vee) Son of Loki and Sigyn,
he was killed by his brother Vali.

NIFLHEIM (*nee*-fl-hime) Realm of ice
and darkness. Hel is in Niflheim.

NIGHT (nite) Mother of Day. She circles
the earth by night.

NORNS (nawns) Three goddesses
concerned with destiny: of Fate, Being
and Necessity.

ODIN (*oh*-din) God. Foremost among
the gods of Asgard. One-eyed. He had
over thirty names. He was god of poets,
warriors and oathbreakers.

OTTER (*ot*-ar) Son of Hreidmar,
killed by Loki.

RAGNAROK (*rag*-nah-*rock*) The great
battle which will destroy the nine worlds.
The Doom of the Gods.

RAN (ran) Goddess. Wife of Aegir,
god of the sea.

REGIN (*ray*-ghin) Son of Hreidmar,
brother of Otter and Fafnir.

RINGHORN (ring-horn)
Balder's funeral boat.

SIGYN (*sig*-in) Goddess. Wife of Loki.

SKIRNIR (*skeer*-near) Freyr's messenger.

SKOLL (skoll) Wolf. He pursues the sun and will swallow it before Ragnarok, the end of the world.

SLEIPNIR (*slipe*-near) Eight-legged horse born to Loki and the stallion Svadilfari and given to Odin. Swiftest horse on earth.

SUN (sun) Daughter of Mundilfari. She drives the sun.

SURT (sert) Giant and flame demon who defeats Freyr at Ragnarok and then sets the world alight. Guardian of Muspell.

SVADILFARI (svad-ill-*far*-ee) Stallion belonging to the giant who offers to rebuild the wall round Asgard. Father of Sleipnir, the eight-legged horse.

THIASSI (thy*ah*-zee) Storm Giant who turns himself into an eagle and kidnaps the goddess Idun and steals her apples of eternal youth.

THOKK (thock) Giantess who refuses to weep for Balder. Thought to be Loki in disguise.

THOR (thaw) Hot tempered Thunder God who owns the hammer Mjolnir. Son of Odin and second only to his father among the gods of Asgard.

THRYM (thrim) Giant who steals Thor's hammer, Mjolnir.

THRYMHEIM (*thrim*-hime) Home of the giant Thiassi.

TYR (tier) Brave god. Son of Odin. Loses one of his hands to the wolf Fenrir.

VALHALLA (val-*halla*) Hall of Odin in Asgard where warriors who are killed in battle live, feasting and fighting until Ragnarok.

VALI (*vah*-lee) Son of Loki and Sigyn. Turned into a wolf which killed his brother, Narvi.

VE (vay) Son of Bor. Brother of Odin and Vili.

VIDAR (*vee*-dar) Son of Odin who avenges his father's death by killing Fenrir the wolf. Survives Ragnarok.

VIGRID (*vigg*-rid) Plain in Asgard where the final battle, Ragnarok, takes place.

VILI (*vi*-lli) Son of Bor. Brother of Odin and Ve. Survives Ragnarok.

YGGDRASIL (*igg*-dra-sill) The World-Tree, an ash which links and shelters the nine worlds and endures for ever.

YMIR (*im*-meer) Giant made in Ginnungagap from ice and fire. The first giant. The world was made from the parts of his body after he was killed.